Miracle
A Birthday Story

written and illustrated by Wendy Alyson Jordan

Archway Publishing books may be ordered through booksellers or by contacting:

Archway Publishing
1663 Liberty Drive
Bloomington, IN 47403
www.archwaypublishing.com
844-669-3957

Interior Image Credit: Wendy Jordan

ISBN: 978-1-6657-2971-0 (sc)
ISBN: 978-1-6657-2970-3 (hc)
ISBN: 978-1-6657-2972-7 (e)

Print information available on the last page.

Archway Publishing rev. date: 10/21/2022

Dedication

With Love and Gratitude for Fritzi.

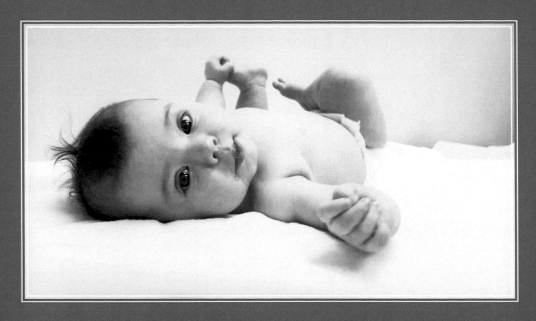

It is Springtime at HeavenWood.

Two weeks ago, a Bison mommy named Sugar Baby had a Baby Bull, we named him Elon.

Today a new baby Bison is born to a very young mommy named Blossom.
On the day she was born it was sunny and bright and early in the morning.

The grass was cool with dew and sparkling in the light of a new day.

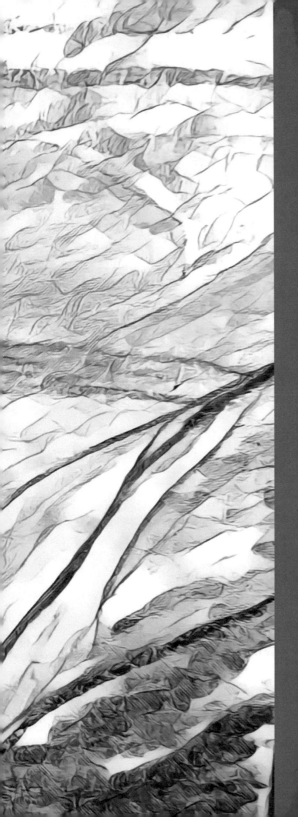

The dragonflies were sipping the dew as their morning coffee.

The ducks were entering
the frog pond.

PLOP! She hit the grassy ground with a sudden thud!

She opened her BIG
Brown EYES and saw
the color of blue sky,
green grass, and the
unfamiliar brightness
of the sunshine.

It's a whole new place with new sounds and smells, different than anything she had sensed before. It wasn't the soft, warm place where she grew for 9 months. It was hard but bright and exciting and full of life.

Can you believe it? She started 9 months
ago from a tiny speck of DNA,
A Map of an American Buffalo! She is an Original.

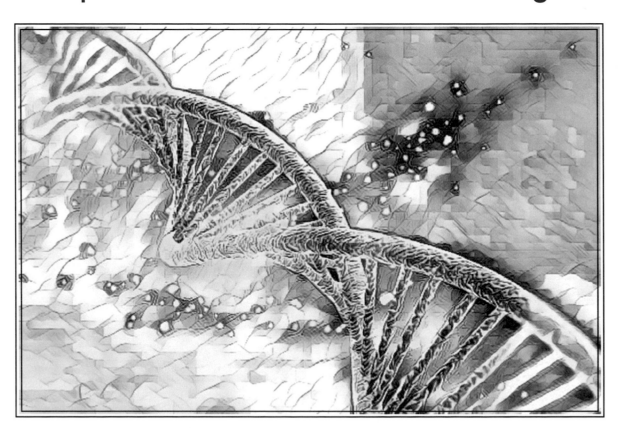

Her birthday will be different than the other
baby Bison born at HeavenWood,
A mom named Blossom gave us a gift we
can touch and feel and love as our own.

First, she is brought to a new place
where she meets Rachel.

Rachael will be her mom, Rachel holds her close, she loves her and feeds her from a bottle every day.

Today she is only 1 day old and she has a limp and a sore knee, Rachel asks the doctor what she can do. Rachel loves her more than anyone, what will happen to her new little baby? Everyone at HeavenWood is worried about our new baby Bison, will she be okay?

Doctor Featherstone had very bad news, Miracle has a fever and needs medicine. He had seen this before and because she is a wild Bison, he does not think she will survive this infection. It is up to us to keep trying to love her through, we believed this baby will survive and thrive because of her new family, the doctor said it would take a Miracle.

We named our Baby Bison, Miracle.

Each day, Rachel feeds Miracle goat milk, she holds her close and sleeps nearby every night for 3 weeks. Miracle knows she is loved by everyone at HeavenWood.

Miracle has new and curious, tall friends and they have four legs too, she shares her home with 4 horses and 2 ponies. They are nearby watching her in the paddock every day, they come to adore and love her too. Miracle has a big new family.

Miracle has a herd, there is Hidalgo, Pee Dee, Choices, Jewels, Napoleon and Nick, they are with Miracle day and night and she can run and play with them, they stay close and she is never lonely.

Each day Miracle grows and learns that different animals have the same needs as her, they need love and a family and a place to call home.

Miracle is embraced by all that see her, she is the Bravest, the Strongest, and the Most Special of all the Bison born at HeavenWood.

Adopting and being adopted is
a beautiful birthday gift!

Epilogue

"Miracle is truly a miracle! Surviving the abandonment, fighting the infections, and then allowing herself to be loved and adopted by humans is called successfully battling the odds….." Jonathan Featherstone, DVM

Printed in the United States
by Baker & Taylor Publisher Services